CAREFUL RAPTURE

A Comedy in One Act

by

JACK POPPLEWELL

SAMUEL FRENCH

LONDON

NEW YORK   TORONTO   SYDNEY   HOLLYWOOD

ESSEX COUNTY LIBRARY

CHARACTERS

(in the order of their appearance)

PEGGY BOWERS
LAURA, her aunt
JOAN BOWERS, her mother
TED DESMOND
BARBARA JANE
MRS BLACKETT

The action of the Play passes in the living-room of the Bowers' home in an English town

SCENE I
Afternoon

SCENE II
Evening. A week later

Time—the present

CAREFUL RAPTURE

SCENE I

SCENE—*The living-room of the Bowers' home in an English town. Afternoon.*

The Bowers are a very ordinary family and the room is neat and tasteful, but not expensive. A door back C *leads to the hall, the front door off* R *and other parts of the house off* L. *A door* L *leads to the kitchen. There is a window* R *overlooking the front garden and street. The fireplace is presumed to be in the "fourth wall". A comfortable sofa is* RC *and an easy chair to match stands* LC. *There is a fireside chair down* R. *A table with a record-player on it is in front of the window and there is a small dining-table up* LC *with chairs* R, L *and above it. There is a footstool or low pouffe in front of the sofa. A standard lamp is in the corner up* R. *Other suitable dressing may be added at the discretion of the Producer.*

When the CURTAIN *rises,* PEGGY BOWERS *is reclining on the sofa, reading a woman's magazine. She is aged nineteen, is very "modern". She wears tight-fitting slacks and jumper. The record-player is blaring out a tune of the day, the beat of the rhythm section causing* PEGGY *to swing her legs in sympathy.* LAURA, *Peggy's aunt enters up* C. *She is middle-aged.*

LAURA. Would you like a cup of tea?

PEGGY (*without looking up*) I can't hear you.

LAURA (*louder*) Would you like a cup of tea?

PEGGY. I still can't hear you.

LAURA (*loudly*) Would you like a . . . ? (*She frowns, goes to the record-player and switches it off*)

PEGGY (*sitting up*) Oh, now look what you've done. Turn it on again.

Laura (*crossing to* L *of the sofa*) I couldn't hear a word you were saying.

Peggy. That's what I said to you. I was reading, anyway.

Laura. You couldn't possibly read and listen to that noise at one and the same time. (*She moves to the easy chair* LC *and sits*) Besides, it's time you were getting ready.

Peggy. Getting ready for what?

Laura. Your young man's coming, isn't he?

Peggy. Only to meet mother. I don't have to dress up for Ted.

Laura. You look terrible. When I was your age the only trousers I wore were kept out of sight. You'll frighten him away.

Peggy (*rising*) He's seen me in these before. (*She parades*) Don't you like them?

Laura. No, I don't. It's all sex-provoking nowadays. Look at you! "Come hither" eye shadow, expensive cheap paint all over you, foundation garments to pull you in, brassières to push you out . . . All set to music that sounds like a jungle. It scares me to death.

Peggy (*sitting on the sofa*) You're off the map!

Laura. I dare say. Well, if you want your young man to see you looking like that, I suppose it's your own affair.

Peggy. I say, Aunt Laura, didn't mother tell you? He isn't a young man.

Laura. Your mother never tells me anything. Who isn't a young man?

Peggy. My young man.

Laura. If your young man isn't a young man, what is he?

Peggy. Forty.

Laura. He's what?

Peggy. Forty. But he doesn't look it. He looks a lot younger. I mean—oh, well, he has young ideas.

Laura. He must have. I suppose you're one of them. What does your mother think?

Peggy. I told her young girls are more mature nowadays. We don't like callow boys our own age. Look at the film stars—they're all in the fifties, aren't they?

LAURA. They were in the fifties in the forties when I was in my twenties.

PEGGY. Ted's very sweet. You feel you want to mother him.

LAURA. You can't mother a man who's old enough to be your father.

PEGGY. Do you know why he never got married before? Mothers-in-law! He says he saw his friends get married and all their marriages were ruined by mothers-in-law. So he swore he'd never have one.

LAURA. He'll have one if he marries you.

PEGGY. He's terrified of meeting mother. That's a laugh! Anyway, he's reserving judgement until they meet. *She's* on trial—not me.

LAURA. So is he. If we don't like him—he's out. Is he very handsome?

PEGGY. No.

LAURA. Dashing?

PEGGY (*giggling*) No.

LAURA. Rich?

PEGGY (*laughing*) No.

LAURA. Well, what's the attraction?

PEGGY. He's just my Ted and he's pleasant.

LAURA. Well, that's comforting, I must say. When did he propose?

PEGGY. Yesterday. I don't know how it happened, really. He said he's often thought of getting married—except, as I said before, for mothers-in-law. Then he said, "I suppose nobody'd want me now". I said, "Oh, lots of girls would marry you." He said, "At my age?" I said, "*Certainly.*" He said, "You mean I'm attractive to women?" and I said, "*Certainly.*" He said, "There's one girl I know who's nine-teen years old. Do you think she'd marry me?" I said, "*Certainly.*" So he took my hand in his, took a deep breath and said, "That's settled, then." (*She shrugs helplessly*) And I said . . .

LAURA. "*Certainly.*"

PEGGY. That's right.

LAURA. What are you going to do about it?

PEGGY. Get married. We can try it, I expect, just for a few years . . .

LAURA (*ironically*) If he isn't satisfactory you can send him back to the manufacturers, can't you?

PEGGY. Oh, well, you know what I mean.

(*The front-door bell rings*)

(*She jumps up*) Good Lord, he's here already.

(PEGGY *exits up* C *to* R, *leaving the door open.*

LAURA *rises, goes to the door up* C, *peeks off* R, *then exits hurriedly up* C *to* L.

TED DESMOND *enters up* C *from* R.

PEGGY *follows him on.* TED *is aged forty-three, and is very shy and nervous. He wears a duffle coat and carries a bowler hat*)

Let me take your hat and coat. (*She takes Ted's hat*)

(TED *removes his coat and hands it to Peggy*)

Sit down, Ted.

(PEGGY *goes into the hall to deposit the hat and coat*)

(*As she goes*) My word, you are early.

TED (*sitting in the easy chair* LC) I thought I was late.

PEGGY (*off*) We said five o'clock.

TED. I thought we said four.

(PEGGY *enters from the hall*)

PEGGY (*as she enters*) I'll tell mother you're here.

TED (*jumping to his feet*) Your mother?

PEGGY (*moving to him*) Well, you want to meet her, don't you?

TED. No. I mean, yes. Look, if I'm too early I can go away and come back again.

PEGGY. Why should you do that?

TED (*resuming his seat*) I don't know.

PEGGY. It's this mother-in-law business, isn't it?

(TED *nods*)

(*She moves close to him*) You've got a complex, that's what you've got. I'm sure she'll like you.

TED. Yes, but shall I like her? (*He takes Peggy's hand*) I told you, I had four friends—they used to call us the four musketeers . . .

PEGGY. Three musketeers.

TED. No, there were four of us.

PEGGY. If you'd four friends there must have been five of you.

TED. Well, anyway, all of them got married. Jim's mother-in-law had a voice like a ship's siren. She broke up the marriage in six months. Tom's was a little woman—(*he gestures*) about so big—but what a personality! Horrible! Lasted three months. Timothy's had a face like an all-in wrestler. That one only lasted a few weeks. So I always said I'd never get engaged to be married unless I'd seen my future wife's mother first.

PEGGY (*moving up* C) Well, I'll tell her you're here.

TED (*rising*) Don't rush her. I can wait.

PEGGY. There's no need to be nervous.

TED. No? You didn't see Timothy before he committed suicide.

PEGGY (*annoyed*) My mother isn't like that at all.

TED. No, I'm sure she isn't.

(PEGGY *exits up* C)

(*He nervously paces the floor, speaking to himself*) You're a fool, Ted Desmond, that's what you are. She's very nice, and it's time you settled down, but . . . Oh, dear! (*He crosses to* LC)

(PEGGY *and* JOAN BOWERS *enter up* C. JOAN, *who is middle-aged, is singularly sweet, pleasant and everything nice*)

PEGGY (*moving down* C) Here he is, Mother. This is Ted.

JOAN (*smiling a welcome*) Hello. (*She moves below the sofa*)

PEGGY (*introducing*) Ted Desmond—my mother.

TED. How do you do?

JOAN (*sitting on the sofa*) Please sit down. Here—beside me.

TED. Thank you. (*He crosses and sits* L *of Joan on the sofa*)

JOAN. Peggy says you smoke a pipe. Please do if you want to.

(PEGGY *sits in the easy chair* LC)

TED. Thank you. (*He takes out his pouch and pipe*)

JOAN. She also says you're thinking of getting married.

TED (*fumbling with his pouch and pipe*) That's right.

JOAN. Don't you think nineteen is a little young for marriage?

TED. That's nice of you, Mrs Bowers, but I'm not nineteen. I'm forty-two.

JOAN. I was referring to Peggy.

(JOAN *and* PEGGY *laugh.* TED *joins in their laughter at his mistake*)

TED. I thought you meant me. Oh, dear!

JOAN. I've looked forward to meeting you, Ted. I'm so glad you were able to come to tea.

TED. Thank you.

JOAN. So you're forty-two and you feel it's time you took a wife. Is that it?

TED (*nodding*) You get tired of doing your own sewing and cooking and washing, you know.

PEGGY (*appalled*) Oh, do you?

JOAN. I suppose whilst you're cooking for one you think you might as well be cooking for two.

TED. Who? Me? (*He smiles*) You're pulling my leg. Anyway, I'm quite a good cook if it comes to that.

JOAN. It will come to that, because Peggy can't even serve a packet of cornflakes.

PEGGY. Of course I can. (*Thoughtfully*) That's about all, though.

TED. She's joking. I think we shall manage.

JOAN. Of course you will. You can send the washing to the laundry, can't you?

TED. Won't that be expensive?

JOAN. And you can always eat in restaurants. What are they there for?

TED. I hadn't seen it quite like that.

JOAN. I often wish Peggy was more domesticated, but I suppose she'll improve with practice. Do you hope to have many children?

TED. I hadn't got as far as that.

PEGGY. Not for the first ten years, we're not. I don't intend to be tied down straight off.

TED. Ten years is a long time, isn't it? I'll be fifty.

PEGGY. You'll be fifty-two.

TED. I'll be fifty-three. I've just remembered—it was my birthday last week.

PEGGY. Many happy returns.

JOAN. We're getting ahead of ourselves, aren't we?

PEGGY. You'll be arguing next whether the children are going to join the army or the navy. (*She rises*) I must go and get the tea ready. (*She moves to the door* L) I shan't be long, Ted dear. Be patient and, above all, be brave.

(PEGGY *exits* L)

TED. Mrs Bowers . . .

JOAN. Call me "Mother". You might as well get used to it straight away.

TED (*realizing the absurdity*) I'd rather call you "Mrs Bowers".

JOAN. Well, then, call me "Joan".

TED. Yes, well . . . Honestly—can't she cook?

JOAN. Not yet. But she'll soon learn. You don't want to get married immediately, do you?

TED. At my age you don't think in terms of long engagements.

JOAN. Two or three years, perhaps?

TED. To be quite honest, Mrs Bowers——

JOAN. Please call me "Joan".

TED. —Joan—I'm sick to death of being in lodgings. I've reached a time of life when a man wants a bit of comfort.

JOAN. Pipe and slippers.

TED. Exactly.

JOAN. A nice, quiet, orderly routine.

TED. That's it.

JOAN. To come home from work and be greeted by a smiling face. A nice meal ready. Then pipe and slippers and a cosy evening by the fire. And at eleven o'clock, lights out.

TED. You've got it just right.

JOAN (*quietly*) With a nineteen-year-old girl?

TED. What's that?

JOAN. You don't suppose she's in that mellow mood at nineteen, do you?

TED. I never thought about it. Actually, I don't know how it happened. I was talking to Peggy. I said, "I'd like to get married. If it wasn't that I'm frightened of mothers-in-law," I said, "I would get married." Well, she looked coy and said, "My mother's very nice." Then I said, "Who'd look twice at a man like me?" And she said, "I would." That could only mean one thing, couldn't it? So I said, "Well, that's settled, then." And as far as I know, she nodded and said, "Certainly".

JOAN. How very romantic!

TED. Yes.

JOAN. I do feel, though, if a man's sufficiently in love with a girl to want to marry her, he shouldn't let her mother stand in his way—however terrible he thinks she is.

TED. I don't know about that, but I was scared of meeting you. I don't mind admitting it.

JOAN. And am I so awful?

TED. Oh, no. I expected some old battle-axe about sixty-five years old.

JOAN. With a daughter of nineteen?

TED. Well, I mean one who looked as if she'd lived sixty-five years and hated every one of them. But you're not like that. You're not like it at all.

JOAN. I should hope not.

TED. You're very nice.

JOAN. Thank you.

TED. If I'd known you were so nice I'd have married Peggy ten years ago.

JOAN. You might have had to wait a little while. She was only nine years old, then.

TED (*laughing*) You've got a great sense of humour.

JOAN. Tell me about yourself, Ted. What do you do for a living?

TED (*very seriously*) Kiosks.

JOAN. I beg your pardon?

TED. Kiosks. I've opened three little tobacco kiosks.

JOAN. Oh, those little round things. I know.

TED. I'm doing very well. I put a girl in each one and they sell tobacco, lighters, postcards and so on.

JOAN. Really! What sort of postcards?

TED. Er—views. Portraits. You know.

JOAN. Oh, yes. I do know. Is Peggy going into one of the kiosks?

TED. No. She says she gets claustrophobia. She says she won't work in a place where every time she turns round she bumps her behind on the counter.

JOAN. Before I got married I worked in a big store.

TED (*pleased*) Did you?

(JOAN *nods*)

You know the ropes, then?

JOAN. Of course.

TED. Well, fancy that!

JOAN. I had to give it up when Peggy came along. I've been a widow for ten years, you know.

TED. I can't think why an attractive woman like you never married again.

JOAN. Oh, I probably will, one of these days.

(LAURA *enters up* C)

TED. I should think so.

JOAN. Oh! (*She introduces Laura*) This is my sister—Peggy's Aunt Laura.

(TED *rises*)

LAURA. How do you do?

TED. Delighted.

LAURA (*to Joan*) Where's Peggy?

JOAN. Preparing the tea.

LAURA (*amazed*) Preparing the tea! Why, she's never . . .

JOAN (*breaking in quickly*) Isn't it exciting meeting Peggy's boy friend for the first time?

TED (*ruefully*) Well, I'm not exactly a boy.

LAURA (*moving to the easy chair* LC *and sitting*) No—you're not, are you?

(PEGGY *enters* L *and crosses to* C)

PEGGY (*to Joan*) Where do we keep the tea-caddy?

JOAN. Usual place, dear.

PEGGY. Where's that?

LAURA. In the cupboard over the sink.

PEGGY. Oh. I'll be with you in a moment, Ted.

(TED *and* PEGGY *smile awkwardly at each other*)

(*She moves to the door* L *then stops and turns*) Oh, how do you light the new eye-level gas stove?

JOAN. Oh, dear!

LAURA. At eye-level, you will find a large knob with the words "ON" and "OFF" printed on it. Turn it to the "ON" position, dear. Then, at hip-level, you will find a row of four taps. Choose one. Turn it on, the gas lights itself and you're in business.

PEGGY. That's handy! When we're married, Ted, we must get one of those. It will save me striking matches.

(PEGGY *exits* L. TED *reacts and resumes his seat.* JOAN *forces a smile*)

JOAN (*to Laura*) Ted is in lodgings. That's why he's decided to get married. He wants all the comforts of a home.

LAURA. There's nothing like home cooking.

TED. That's right. The quickest way to a man's heart is through his stomach.

LAURA (*with meaning*) That depends. It can also be the quickest way to the cemetery.

(PEGGY *enters* L)

Peggy. How long do you boil an egg?

(Ted's *eyes pop out*)

Is it ten minutes?

Ted (*jumping to his feet*) Ten minutes?

(Joan *smiles and persuades* Ted *to resume his seat*)

Laura (*to Peggy*) Don't bother with anything fancy, dear. (*To Ted*) She's trying to show off. (*To Peggy*) Just do something simple.

Peggy. Oh, all right.

(Peggy *exits* L *but re-enters immediately*)

Where's the tin-opener?

Joan. In the top left-hand drawer.

Peggy. I'll be with you in a moment, Ted dear.

(Peggy *and* Ted *smile nervously at each other.*
Peggy *exits* L. *There is an awkward silence*)

Laura (*breaking the silence*) It's very warm for the time of the year, isn't it?

Ted. Yes, it is.

(*A deafening clatter of pans falling to the floor is heard off in the kitchen.*
Ted *jumps up and rushes out* L *to assist Peggy.* Joan *and* Laura *smile at each other*)

Joan. This tea's going to be really something.

Laura. Wait until he sees the sandwiches.

Joan. Yes, I know.

Laura. Joan, I know you told me to leave Peggy to get the tea, but I thought you were pulling my leg. She's hopeless and helpless. Why, she's never raised a finger to help you in the home.

Joan. He wants good cooking and all the comforts of home life. He has a right to a preview of what he's in for.

Laura. You mean you're trying to put him off?

Joan. Of course. I'm trying to put them *both* off. Ted

is easy. It's a simple matter to convince him there's something wrong with his supposed love match—as you can see
—but I shall have to be more diplomatic with Peggy. You
wouldn't think so, but she's pretty sensitive. Also, the more
you push her, the more she resists. I've somehow got to
succeed without hurting anyone.

LAURA. How do you propose to do it?

JOAN. You'll see, but let's continue to convince Ted first
of all. I telephoned Barbara Jane and invited her round
for tea.

LAURA. Who's Barbara Jane?

JOAN. Peggy's friend. The one she calls "Barb".

LAURA. Not that awful teenager?

JOAN. That's the one.

LAURA. Why?

JOAN. Ted ought to meet the other young people,
shouldn't he? They're his future friends. She's a typical
example. There are some forty-year-olds who are at home
with teenagers—those who never grow up—but he isn't like
that.

LAURA. He'll grow up so fast in their company he'll be
prematurely old inside two years.

JOAN. He's rather sweet, isn't he?

LAURA. He'd have been a better match for her twenty
years ago.

JOAN. I know. Except she hadn't been born, then.

LAURA. He might be all right for me.

(JOAN *reacts*)

Well, I'm in his age group, aren't I?

JOAN. I never heard anything so immoral—to compete
with your own niece.

LAURA. Oh, they won't go through with it. They only
found themselves in it because they got mixed up in a con-
versation neither of them understood. When they've un-
ravelled it, it will all be over and done with.

(*The sound of breaking crockery is heard off in the kitchen*)

She's hurling the crockery at him already.

(Peggy *enters* l)

Peggy. Have we got another teapot?

Joan. Oh, dear! What's happened now? I know—it fell. There's another in the cupboard over the fridge.

(Peggy *exits* l.
Ted *enters* l, *nursing his hand*)

Ted (*crossing to* c) I'm afraid I dropped it. I'm terribly sorry.

Joan. Don't worry. Sit down, Ted.

(Ted *sits* l *of Joan on the sofa*)

Ted. It was careless of me. I'm very sorry.

Laura. What happened?

Ted. Peggy was pouring the hot water into it.

Laura. When you were holding it?

Ted. That's right. I thought she'd pour it into the pot, but she didn't. She missed.

Laura. And it went all over your hand?

Ted. That's right.

Joan. Oh, you poor man! You're scalded! .

Ted. It's nothing. Luckily for me she hadn't let the water boil. Letting go of that teapot was the fastest thing I've done in years.

(Joan *examines Ted's hand*)

Joan. How painful it must be.

Ted. It's nothing—really.

Joan. You have a strong hand. A real man's hand.

Ted. Have I?

Joan. Oh, yes. Strong and masculine, yet sensitive and artistic.

Ted (*surprised*) Is it? I didn't know I was artistic.

Joan. Didn't you really?

Ted. No. Honestly.   .

Joan. I can't believe that. (*To Laura*) Can you?

Laura (*dryly*) I can believe anything.

(Peggy *enters* l, *carrying a tray with tea things for five, a plate with a chocolate cake and a plate of large, crusty, "door-step" ham sandwiches. As she enters, the cake slides from its plate to the floor.* Ted *rises.* Peggy *puts the tray on the table up* lc.

TED *picks up the cake from the floor and stands awkwardly holding it*)

PEGGY. Come and get it!

LAURA. You do it so delicately, dear.

PEGGY (*to Ted*) What are you holding that for?

TED. It was on the floor.

PEGGY (*picking up the cake plate*) Well, put it on here.

(TED *puts the cake on the plate*)

(*She puts the plate on the table*) Now, sit down again.

(TED *crosses and sits on the chair down* R. PEGGY *gives each of them a cup and saucer*)

LAURA. May I have a plate, please?

PEGGY. Oh, yes. (*She gives each of them a small plate, then picks up the plate of sandwiches and offers them to Laura and Joan*)

(LAURA *and* JOAN *take a sandwich.* PEGGY *offers the sandwiches to* TED. *It is difficult for* TED *to take one, as each hand is already occupied. He finally manages to take one huge, crusty sandwich which he surveys in puzzlement*)

JOAN. There we are. Isn't this nice?

(PEGGY *replaces the sandwiches on the table and picks up the teapot*)

LAURA. What dainty sandwiches!

(TED *tussles toothfully, but vainly, with his sandwich. The others watch the enormous struggle for some time. He is unable to bite it and smiles unhappily*)

TED. What's in this sandwich?

PEGGY (*crossing to Ted with the teapot*) Tinned ham.

TED. Are you sure you took it out of the tin?

PEGGY. Tea?

TED. I think I've lost my appetite.

(*Another catastrophe occurs.* PEGGY *pours liquid into Ted's cup, over his knee and down his legs.* TED *gives a howl of pain, drops everything and stands up. After considerable howling he looks thoughtfully at Peggy*)

Peggy (*casually*)   Sorry!   (*She pours tea into Joan's and Laura's cups*)

(Joan *and* Laura *stare at the tea*)

Laura.   It's a little pale, isn't it?

Peggy.   Oh, dear, I must have forgotten to put tea in the pot.   (*She puts the teapot on the tray*)

Joan.   Don't worry, dear.   It's nice and hot.

Ted.   I don't know about nice, but it's hot.

Peggy.   You haven't eaten your sandwich.

Ted.   I'm not very hungry.   I'm all wet.

Joan (*touching Ted's leg*)   He is, too.   He's soaking.   Oh, dear, what shall we do with him?

Laura.   Can't he wear something of Brian's?

Ted.   Who's Brian?

Peggy.   My young brother.   Yes, you can put on something of his.   You're not the same size, but I don't suppose it will matter.

(Joan *puts her cup and plate on the floor beside her and rises*)

Joan.   That's a good idea.

Peggy.   Come on, Ted.

Ted.   Oh, all right.

Peggy (*giggling*)   You do look soppy.

Ted.   "Soppy" 's the right word.

Peggy.   I can't help laughing, but I'm sorry I poured the tea over you.

Ted.   It's nothing, really.   The skin will grow again.

Peggy.   Well, of course, if you're going to take it the wrong way . . .

Joan.   I'll take care of him, dear.   (*To Ted*)   Let's go to Brian's room and see what we can find, shall we?

(Joan *and* Ted *exit up* c)

Peggy (*to Laura*)   Drop more tea?

Laura.   Are you kidding?   You know, Peggy, the normal way of breaking off an engagement is to say "Take your ring back", not to pour hot water over the poor man.

Peggy (*unconvincingly*)   Oh, so that's what you think, is it?   Well, that's very unfair.   I like Ted very much.

LAURA. You're supposed to love him.

PEGGY. All right, well—I do love him, then. And nothing's going to stop my marrying him. Now that he's seen mother, and likes her, we shall go straight ahead.

LAURA. But you're not properly engaged yet, are you? Has he bought the ring?

PEGGY. Yes. A lovely emerald. But he wanted to see mother first. If he didn't like her, it was off.

LAURA (*thoughtfully*) But he does like her.

PEGGY. He thinks she's wonderful.

LAURA. Yes . . .

PEGGY. All the time we were together in the kitchen he was telling me how nice she is. In fact, with any encouragement, I could be jealous. Silly—a daughter being jealous of her own mother.

LAURA (*meaningly*) Yes, dear.

> (*The front-door bell rings.*
>   PEGGY *exits up* C *to* R.
>   BARBARA JANE *enters up* C *from* R. PEGGY *follows her on.*
> BARBARA *is a bright example of the modern generation and wears whatever is fashionable amongst teenagers*)

PEGGY. You know Barbara Jane, don't you, Aunt Laura?

BARBARA (*deadpan*) Hi!

LAURA. Hi!

BARBARA. Your mother asked me round for tea.

PEGGY. Help yourself to a sandwich.

> (BARBARA *takes a sandwich*)

BARBARA. What did you cut these with—a hack-saw?

PEGGY. Don't be funny!

> (BARBARA *goes to the record-player and starts the music to which she gyrates rhythmically, holding the huge sandwich aloft*)

BARBARA (*to Laura*) I go for this stuff.

LAURA. I'm glad. Somebody should.

BARBARA (*to Peggy*) Where is he?

PEGGY (*moving above the easy chair* LC) Where's who?

BARBARA (*moving below the sofa*) The boy friend. Your mother said . . .

PEGGY. Oh, he's changing his trousers.

BARBARA. I never heard it expressed like that before. Do I know him?

PEGGY. No.

BARBARA. I can't wait to see him. (*She holds up the sandwich*) Can I take this home with me? Our dog will gnaw at it for hours. Is he good-looking? If you're going to get married you might as well have something decent to look at over the breakfast table. If ever I get married my husband will be a lot older than I am. Middle-aged. I don't like boys.

LAURA. Then you'll like Ted. He's middle-aged all right.

BARBARA. How old is he?

LAURA. Forty-three. It was his birthday last week.

BARBARA (*appalled*) Forty-three? You're kidding!

LAURA. You said you liked middle-aged men.

BARBARA. Forty-three isn't middle-age. It's history. I meant about thirty.

PEGGY. Well, he isn't thirty. He's forty-three.

BARBARA. Gee! (*To Peggy*) Am I sorry for you. Where did you find him? The Old People's Home?

LAURA. You'll be surprised. He's still good for five or six years.

BARBARA. When I get married I expect to draw the children's allowance, not an old age pension.

(JOAN *and* TED *enter up* C. TED *wears an ill-fitting pair of jeans and a leather jacket. He is very ill at ease*)

JOAN. There! How does he look now?

BARBARA (*to Peggy*) You don't mean to say this is him?

JOAN. Oh, hello, Barbara. Ted, this is Barbara Jane.

BARBARA. Hi!

TED. Hi! (*He proffers his hand*)

(BARBARA, *instead of shaking Ted's hand, puts the sandwich in it.* TED *reacts then puts the sandwich on the plate*)

JOAN. Laura, why don't we old folks go into the other room and leave the young people together?

LAURA (*surprised*) What? (*Understanding*) Oh, yes, of

course. (*She rises*)

JOAN. I suppose we can wash the tea things.

(*During the next few speeches,* LAURA *and* JOAN *bustle about the room, collecting the tea things and stacking them on the tray. The other three watch*)

What a lot of sandwiches have been left.

LAURA. Yes. I wonder why.

JOAN. I always say there's nothing nicer than a nice cup of tea. Don't you?

LAURA. Oh, yes. I've been saying it for years.

JOAN (*affecting surprise*) Nobody ate any of the chocolate cake.

LAURA. Oh? How surprising!

JOAN. You can turn the music up louder if you want to. Then you can dance together, can't you?

LAURA. Youth must be served.

JOAN. Now then, children, have lots of fun. (*She crosses to the record-player*)

JOAN *turns up the record-player to an ear-splitting din, crosses to the table, picks up the tea tray and goes to the door* L. BARBARA *begins to gyrate to the rhythm of the music and moves towards Ted, urging him to partner her.*

LAURA *and* JOAN *exit* L. TED *reluctantly and awkwardly partners* BARBARA *who is rocking and rolling spiritedly as—*

the CURTAIN *falls*

SCENE II

SCENE—*The same. Evening. A week later.*

When the CURTAIN *rises it is about eight o'clock. The remains of an evening meal are on the table up* LC. *The lights are on, the window curtains are closed and the room looks cosy.* JOAN *is seated* R *of the table and* TED *is seated* L *of it.* TED *finishes the sweet, sighs and puts down his spoon.*

TED. Well, I must say, that's the best meal I've tucked away in years. It was very nice of you to invite me.

JOAN. Nothing of the kind. A little cheese?

TED. Joan, I couldn't eat another thing.

JOAN. Biscuits and cheese and celery hearts to finish off with. Come along.

TED. No. It would finish me off. It really would.

JOAN (*rising*) Very well, then. We'll have coffee by the fire, shall we?

TED. That would be nice. (*He rises*)

(JOAN *motions for Ted to sit on the sofa.* TED *crosses to the sofa and sits.* JOAN *puts a footstool in front of Ted*)

JOAN. Rest your feet on here, Ted.

(TED *rests his feet on the footstool*)

(*Contemplating*) No. Brian's slippers wouldn't fit you. I guess you've had a hard day visiting all those kiosks of yours.

TED. Thank you. Yes, I am tired.

JOAN. Light your pipe. I like to see a man smoking a pipe. It's cosy.

TED. All right. (*He takes out his pipe and pouch*) My goodness, but this is the life. I didn't know I was born.

JOAN. A man has a right to be fussed a little after a hard day's work.

TED. Yes. I think so, too. (*He fills his pipe*)

JOAN. You must be dead on your feet driving round all day in that car of yours, going from one kiosk to another.

TED (*uncertain of her sincerity*) I've only got three of them, you know.

JOAN. With young girls in charge I should think it's a strain on your nerves. I'll fetch the coffee.

(JOAN *exits* L. TED *lights his pipe, stretches his legs and almost purrs with contentment.*

JOAN *re-enters* L *with a tray of coffee for two which she puts on the table up* LC)

TED. This is better than lodgings, you know.

JOAN (*moving* C) I should hope so. You know, Ted, I went round to look at your kiosks the other day.

TED (*surprised*) You did?

JOAN. Well, no, not exactly. I happened to be passing.

TED. Happened to be passing all three of them?

JOAN. At the first one, I asked the girl for a packet of cigarettes. She gave me a packet of ten.

TED. What was wrong with that?

JOAN. Bad salesmanship. She should have given me twenty.

TED. Why?

JOAN. If people just say "a packet", the saleswoman should always make it twenty. More times than otherwise the customer would keep them. That's good for business, isn't it?

TED. My word, that's smart!

JOAN. At another kiosk I asked for a certain make of lighter. The girl looked up from the magazine she was reading and said she hadn't got it in stock.

TED. We can't stock them all.

JOAN. At least she should have said she'd get one for me. And she should have tried to sell me one of those she did have. (*She moves to the table up* LC)

TED. That's right. She should.

JOAN (*picking up the coffee-pot*) Black or white?

TED. What's that? Oh—white, please.

(JOAN *pours the coffee and takes a cup to* Ted)

JOAN. There you are.

TED. Thank you.

(JOAN (*offers sugar*)

(*He helps himself to sugar*) I can see I shall have to take you in as my partner.

JOAN (*collecting her coffee*) You could do worse.

TED. You've got good ideas. You'd be an asset.

(JOAN *sits* L *of Ted on the sofa. They sip their coffee.* TED *chuckles*)

JOAN. Now what's amused you?

TED. I was just thinking. I came here in the first place to look you over. Oh, yes, I did. I was terrified. I don't know how Peggy and I got engaged, but I remember I said I wouldn't put the ring on her finger until I'd seen you.

JOAN. Well?

TED. My future mother-in-law. It's funny, isn't it?

JOAN. Why?

TED. Because I like you better than her. I realized—that day when I came for tea—it wasn't any good. I think she did, too. Jazz and dancing are no use to me, and I'm no use to Peggy.

JOAN. Different generations don't mix very well, do they?

TED. We quarrelled last night.

JOAN. She mentioned it. Just a lovers' tiff, I suppose.

TED. Do you think so? She said, "If you hadn't been too skinny to give me an engagement ring, I'd throw it right in your face." (*He laughs*)

JOAN. But you did buy a ring, didn't you?

TED. Oh, yes. I have it on me now. (*He laughs*) But, as I said before, I meant to hang on until I found what sort of a mother-in-law I was going to get. Because once the ring's on, it's final, isn't it?

JOAN. And then?

TED. I liked you very much, but things didn't seem to go smoothly after that, did they? I think the turning-point was when I came to tea.

JOAN. I suppose it was.

TED. Those sandwiches. That dreadful friend. The cake on the floor. *And* I was scalded in two places. It wasn't exactly a big success, was it?

JOAN. It depends how you look at it.

TED (*surprised*) Does it?

JOAN. Well, if you're thinking of breaking off the engagement, what are your plans for the future?

TED. I haven't any.

JOAN. Oh.

TED. Except to act my age for a change. (*He laughs*) I can't help laughing, though. Me fancying my chances with a young girl. How silly can you get?

JOAN. You were lonely.

Ted. Yes, I know.

Joan. And she was young, flattered by the interest of a suave, mature man of the world.

Ted. Oh, I don't know about that.

Joan. Of course she was. When you proposed she was swept off her feet.

Ted. Was she?

Joan. She accepted you, didn't she? (*She collects Ted's coffee-cup, rises and puts both cups on the table up* LC)

Ted. Yes. But, as I told you, it was more a misunderstanding than anything else. I don't express myself very well. I didn't make it clear to her that I was just thinking aloud. It happened, as you might say, by accident. When we stopped talking I suddenly found I was more or less trapped.

Joan (*laughing*) How funny. (*She resumes her seat on the sofa*)

Ted. I'll keep a sharp look-out in future. It won't happen again, I'll promise you.

Joan. Do you mean you've decided you never *will* get married?

Ted. I'm not sure. Anyway, who'd have me?

Joan. Lots of women would be thrilled to get a man like you.

Ted. That's a likely story.

Joan. Will you be taking the engagement ring back to the shop?

Ted. They won't have it now. It's paid for.

Joan. What a waste! I'd like to see it.

Ted. It's in my pocket somewhere. Here it is. (*He takes a box from his pocket and shows Joan the ring*)

Joan. How beautiful! I love emeralds.

Ted. It cost a lot of money.

Joan (*playfully*) It's so long since I wore one, I've almost forgotten which finger it goes on.

Ted (*pointing*) That one.

Joan. Oh? This one?

Ted. Third finger of the left hand. (*Surprised*) Fancy you forgetting that.

Joan (*taking the ring*) I don't suppose it will fit me. I have thick fingers.

Ted (*outraged*) You certainly haven't got thick fingers.

Joan. Haven't I?

Ted. They're the nicest fingers I've ever seen.

Joan (*trying to put on the ring*) See! It's much too small.

Ted. No, it isn't.

Joan (*smiling sweetly*) I wonder if you can get it to go on.

Ted (*taking the ring*) Of course I can. (*He slips the ring easily on to Joan's finger*) Just needed a bit of patience, that's all. There!

Joan. Ted, the woman who wears this will be a very lucky woman.

Ted. Oh, I don't know. Remember—I go with it.

Joan. That's why she'd be lucky.

Ted (*laughing*) I can't help laughing. I was just thinking. I was frightened of you being my mother-in-law and now—you're wearing my engagement ring. Wouldn't it be funny if we were to get married?

Joan (*without enthusiasm and still playing up to him*) I'd hardly call it funny. (*She rises*) I'm not the woman I was. I'm not young and attractive any more. It's sad, very sad, to grow old.

Ted (*rising*) That's nonsense!

Joan (*without conviction*) Who'd look at me?

Ted. Any man.

Joan. Oh, no, they wouldn't.

Ted (*gallantly*) Oh, yes, they would.

Joan. Look at me. Look into my face. Who'd want to spend the rest of his life looking at that?

Ted (*defiantly*) I would.

Joan. Oh, no, you wouldn't.

Ted. Oh, yes, I would.

Joan. Would you?

Ted. Certainly!

Joan. Ted! How very gallant you are. (*She plants a perfunctory kiss on his forehead then moves away* LC, *hand outstretched, to admire the ring*)

(Laura *and* Peggy *enter up* C)

Laura. I'm tired out. (*She sees Ted*) Oh, hello. (*She sees Joan admiring the ring*) Hel-lo! What's going on?

JOAN (*displaying the ring*) Isn't it beautiful?

PEGGY. What *is* going on?

LAURA. An emerald ring. And I don't think it's been placed there very long, either.

PEGGY (*beginning to see daylight*) But, Mother, that's the ring Ted bought for me.

JOAN. Yes, dear.

LAURA (*without conviction*) Well, I *am* surprised. (*She moves and stands below the table up* LC)

PEGGY. You don't mean to tell me—you and Ted . . . ?

JOAN (*referring to the ring*) Shall we say, it's on approval for the moment.

PEGGY. What! That joke again? Well, you never can tell. Really, Mother! Shouldn't I pull your hair, or scratch your face, or something? Somehow I don't feel like doing any of those things. I've been an idiot, haven't I? (*She crosses to Joan and embraces her*) Thank you, darling.

(*During the embrace*, JOAN, *unseen by* TED, *winks and smiles at Laura, her object achieved.* PEGGY *suddenly turns from Joan to Ted, looks him over for a moment then bursts out laughing*)

JOAN. May we share the joke, dear?

PEGGY. It's *Ted!*

(TED *looks embarrassed*)

Now I'll have to call him "*Daddy*"!

(*All laugh except* TED *who looks even more embarrassed*)

How did it happen—*Daddy?*

TED. I don't know, really.

PEGGY. You never do, do you?

TED. No. You see, we were talking about something or other—I don't remember what it was—when suddenly . . .

(*There is a sudden and prolonged ring at the front-door bell.* PEGGY *moves up* C)

LAURA. I'll go in a second. (*To Ted*) Well, go on. What then?

TED. I just told you—I don't know. (*He smiles*) And I

don't care very much, either. It doesn't matter which way you go—does it—just as long as you get to the right place.

PEGGY (*moving above the sofa*) Good old Teddy.

LAURA. Don't be disrespectful to your future father.

(*The front-door bell rings.* TED, *master of the situation, sits on the sofa and lights his pipe with great authority.*
LAURA *exits up* C *to* R, *leaving the door open*)

MRS BLACKETT (*off; in a stentorian voice*) It took you a long time to open the door, didn't it?

JOAN (*unable to hide her pleasure*) It's mother!

TED (*rising; incredulously*) What, *your* mother?

(MRS BLACKETT *storms in up* C. *She is large, unpleasant, bossy, autocratic, ill-tempered and, indeed, appears to possess every vice Ted has always feared in a mother-in-law.*
LAURA *follows her on and stands up* LC)

MRS BLACKETT (*moving down* C) Let me tell you I'm not used to standing in draughty doorways. Are you all deaf? Didn't you 'ear the bell?

PEGGY. Hullo, Grandma.

MRS BLACKETT (*at a fast pace and hardly pausing for breath*) Don't you "Grandma" me! There's a taxi outside and my bags are in it. (*To Ted*) Fetch them in, you! And do it at the double. The taxi-meter's still ticking.

(TED, *unbelieving, is aghast and does not move*)

(*She turns to Peggy*) You're wearing too much lipstick so you can wipe that off straight away for a start.

(PEGGY *creeps slowly out up* C)

(*To Ted*) And put that filthy pipe away now that I'm 'ere. I don't 'old with dirty 'abits in the 'ouse. It's 'orrible for my asthma.

(PEGGY *enters unobtrusively up* C *carrying Ted's hat and coat. She goes to Ted, gently nudges him and without a word offers him the hat and coat*)

(*She turns to Laura*) You'll 'ave to pay the taxi. My purse is in my suitcase. And don't give 'im a tip. He was insolent.

(Laura *exits up* c *to* r)

What a fug in 'ere!

(Ted, *without further ado, grabs his hat and coat from Peggy and exits quietly and hurriedly up* c *to* r)

It's like a saloon bar on a Saturday night. (*She turns to Joan*) Now that I'm here, I'm not staying for less than a month. (*She turns to speak to Ted*) *My bags!* D'you 'ere me? (*But Ted has already gone*) Oh. 'E's gone!

Peggy. Yes. He's gone. (*She smiles knowingly*) Now you can relax—*both* of you. I'll go and help Aunt Laura with your luggage.

(Peggy *exits up* c *to* r)

Mrs Blackett (*smiling; gently*) You know, Joan, it would serve you right if I *did* stay for a month. You only send for me when you're in trouble. Anyhow, I seem to have timed it well. How was I? Did I overdo it?

Joan. Mother, darling, you always over-act. But never mind. Your entrance was—magnificent.

Curtain

ALTERNATIVE ENDING

(*To Ted*) And put that filthy pipe away now that I'm 'ere. I don't 'old with dirty 'abits in the 'ouse. It's 'orrible for my asthma. (*She turns to Laura*) You'll 'ave to pay the taxi. My purse is in my suitcase. And don't give 'im a tip. He was insolent.

(Laura *exits up* c *to* r)

What a fug in 'ere! It's like a saloon bar on a Saturday night. (*She turns to Joan*) Now that I'm here, I'm not staying for less than a month. (*She turns to speak to Ted*) *My bags!* D'you 'ear me? *At once!*

Curtain

FURNITURE AND PROPERTY LIST

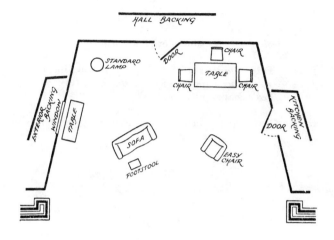

SCENE I

On stage: Sofa. *On it:* cushions, woman's magazine
Easy chair. *On it:* cushion
Fireside chair
Table. *On it:* record-player
Table (up LC)
3 upright chairs
Footstool
Standard lamp
Window curtains
Carpet on floor
Other suitable dressing as desired

Off stage: Tray. *On it:* pot of very weak tea, jug of milk, sugar
basin, 5 cups, 5 saucers, 5 small plates, 5 teaspoons,

plate with chocolate cake, plate with large, crusty
ham sandwiches (PEGGY)

Personal: TED: pouch with tobacco, pipe, matches

SCENE II

Set: *On table up* LC: remains of evening meal

Off stage: Tray.   *On it:* pot of coffee, jug of milk, sugar basin,
2 coffee-cups, 2 saucers, 2 spoons (JOAN)
Ted's coat and hat (PEGGY)

Personal: TED: pipe, pouch with tobacco, matches, box with
emerald ring

LIGHTING PLOT

Property fittings required: standard lamp
 Interior. A living-room. The same scene throughout
 THE MAIN ACTING AREAS are C, at a sofa RC and at an easy
  chair LC
 THE APPARENT SOURCES OF LIGHT are, in daytime, a window
  R; and at night, a standard lamp up R

SCENE I. Afternoon
To open: Effect of sunshine
     Lamp off
No cues

SCENE II Evening
To open: Blue outside window
     Lamp on
No cues

EFFECTS PLOT

SCENE I

Cue 1   At rise of CURTAIN   (Page 1)
Music from record-player

Cue 2   LAURA switches off record-player   (Page 1)
Stop music

Cue 3   PEGGY: ". . . what I mean."   (Page 4)
Front-door bell rings

Cue 4   TED: "Yes, it is."   (Page 11)
Clatter of pans falling to the floor

Cue 5   LAURA: ". . . and done with."   (Page 12)
Sound of breaking crockery

Cue 6   LAURA: "Yes, dear."   (Page 16)
Front-door bell rings

Cue 7   BARBARA switches on record-player   (Page 16)
Start music

Cue 8   JOAN adjusts record-player   (Page 18)
Increase volume of music

SCENE II

Cue 9   TED: ". . . when suddenly . . ."   (Page 24)
Prolonged ring of front-door bell

Cue 10   LAURA: ". . . your future father."   (Page 25)
Front-door bell rings

MADE AND PRINTED IN GREAT BRITAIN BY
LATIMER TREND & COMPANY LTD PLYMOUTH
MADE IN ENGLAND